ABC's with Lighties

By Michael Spencer

Illustrations
with @firstnameryan

Copyright © 2016 Mindsight Publishing
All rights reserved.

Acknowledgements

Special thanks to Ryan Mose (@firstnameryan) for his amazing contributions to the illustrations and design of this book. It would not have been possible without his help and expertise.

Copyright © 2016 Michael Spencer.
All rights reserved. Published by Mindsight Publishing

No part of this book may be reproduced or transmitted in any form or by any means, electronic or mechanical, including photocopying, recording, or by any information storage and retrieval system without written permission from the author or publisher.

For more information contact Mindsight Publishing, P.O. Box 153633, San Diego, CA 92195

ISBN-10:0-9910995-1-6

ISBN-13:978-0-9910995-1-1

Aa

Airplane

Apple

Arrow

Bb

Blimp

Butterfly

Bicycle

Cc

Coconuts

Cabana

Cup

Dd

Dancing

Donut

Diamond

Ee

Easel

Eggplant

Eggs

Ff

Flies

Fan

Fart

Gg

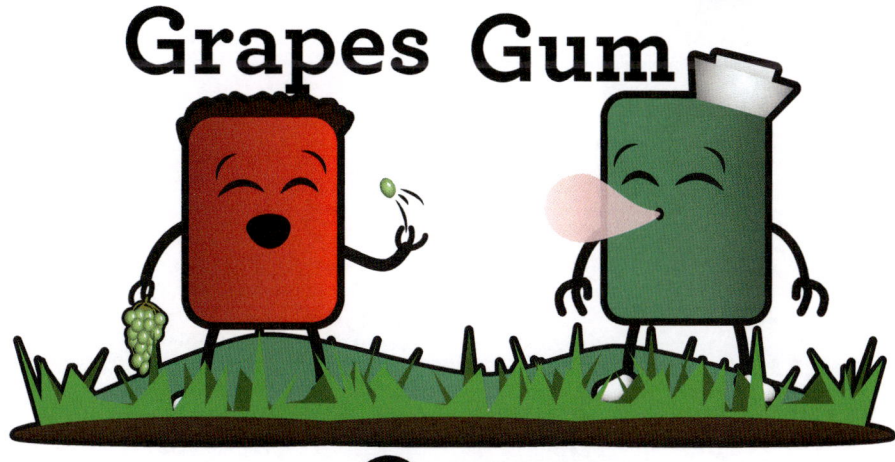

Grapes Gum

Grass

Hh

Hat

Horse

Hay

Ii

Ice cream

Idea

Ink

Jj

Jewels

Juice

Jester

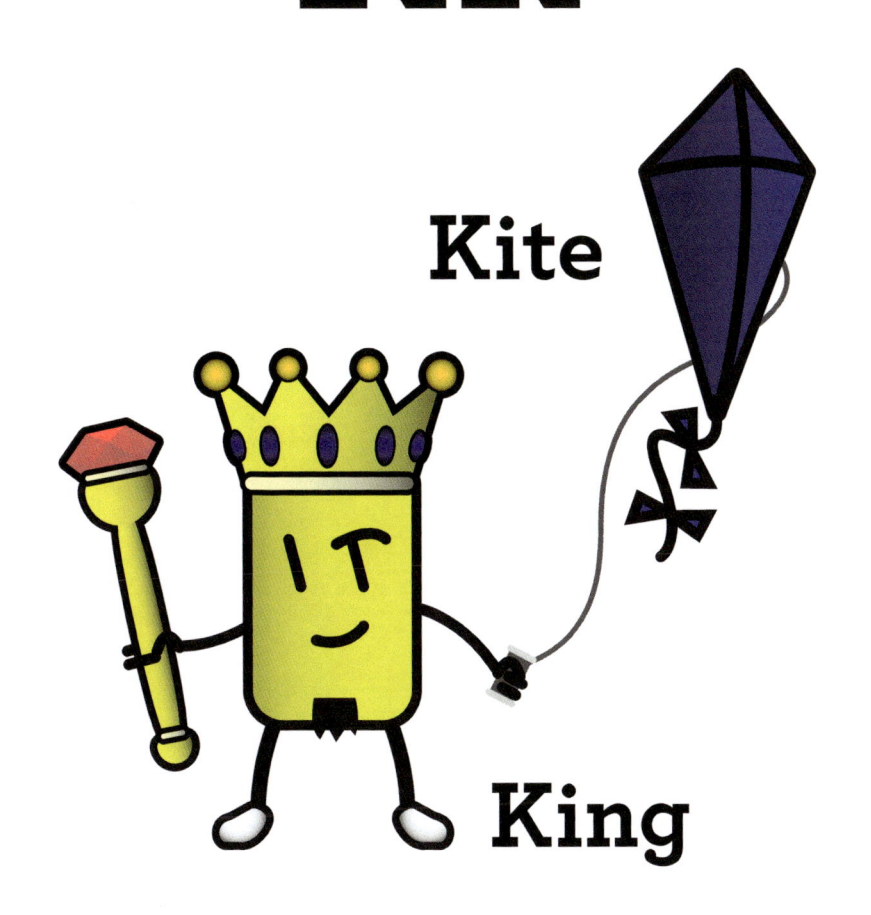

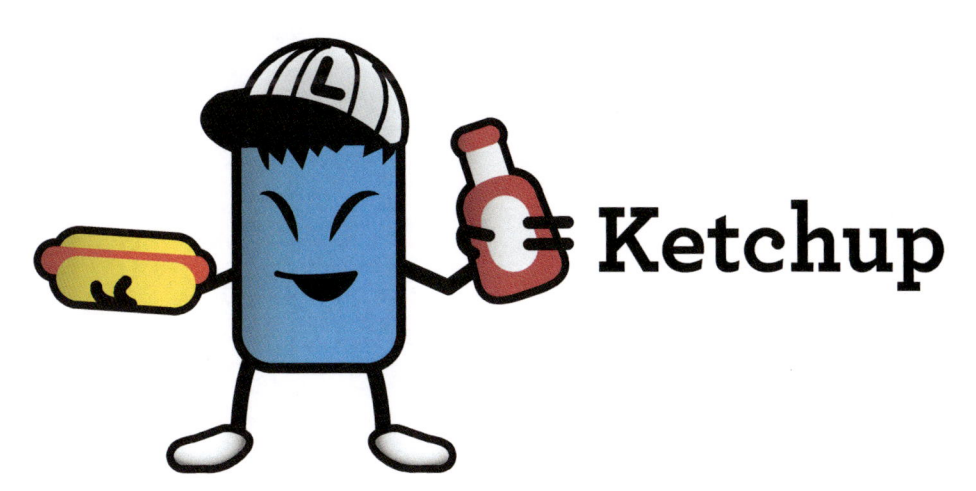

Kk

Kite

King

Ketchup

Ll

Lemonade

Lollilop

Ladybug

Mm

Mitten

Mushrooms

Money

Nn

1 2 3
Numbers

Ninja

Net

Oo

Oranges

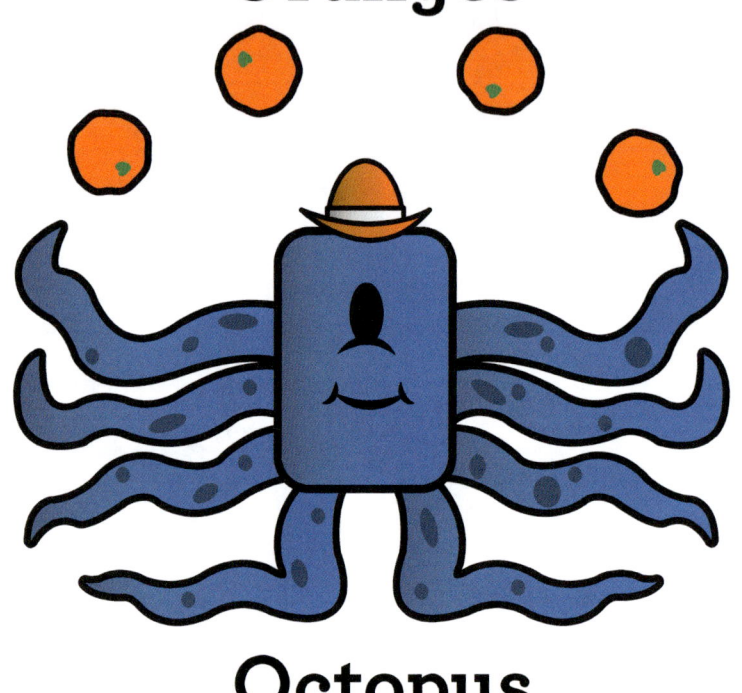

Octopus

Oyster

Pp

Popcorn

Pizza

Pickle

Qq

Question

Queen

Quarterback

Rr

Rattlesnake

Rose

Running

Ss

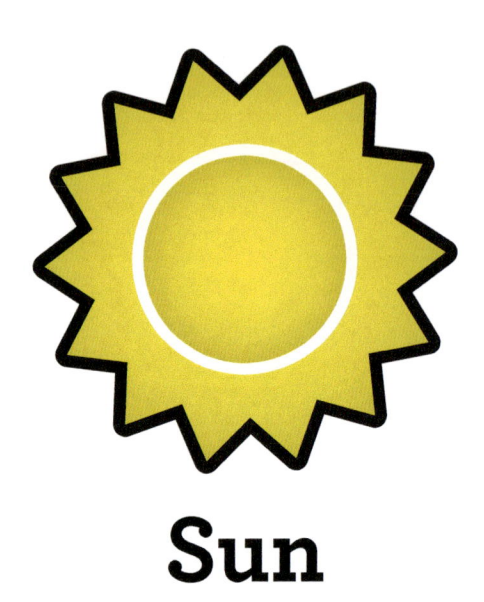

Sun

Sunglasses

Sandals

Starfish

Tt

Tennis Racquet

Tennis Ball

Tie

Turtle

Uu

Umbrella

Unicorn   Unicycle

Vine

Vv

Violin

Vase

Wand

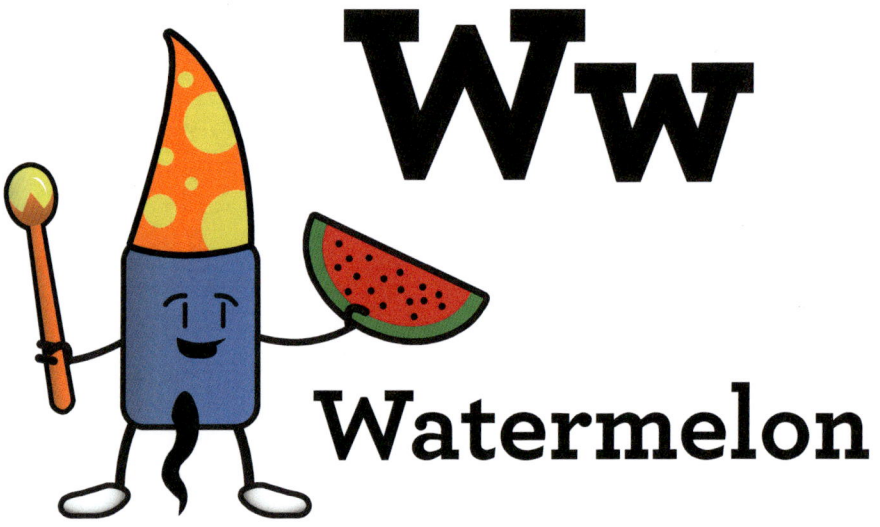

Ww

Watermelon

Wizard

Xx

Xylophone

X-Ray

Xiphias

Yy

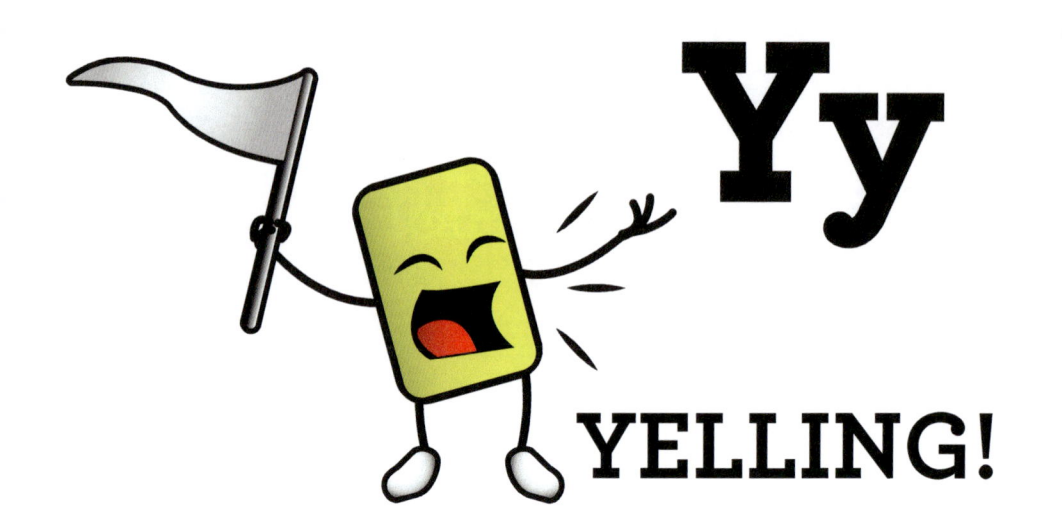

YELLING!

Yo-yo

Yoga

Zz

Zoo

Zoom!

Zero

Now you know your ABC's.
Thanks for learning with Lighties!

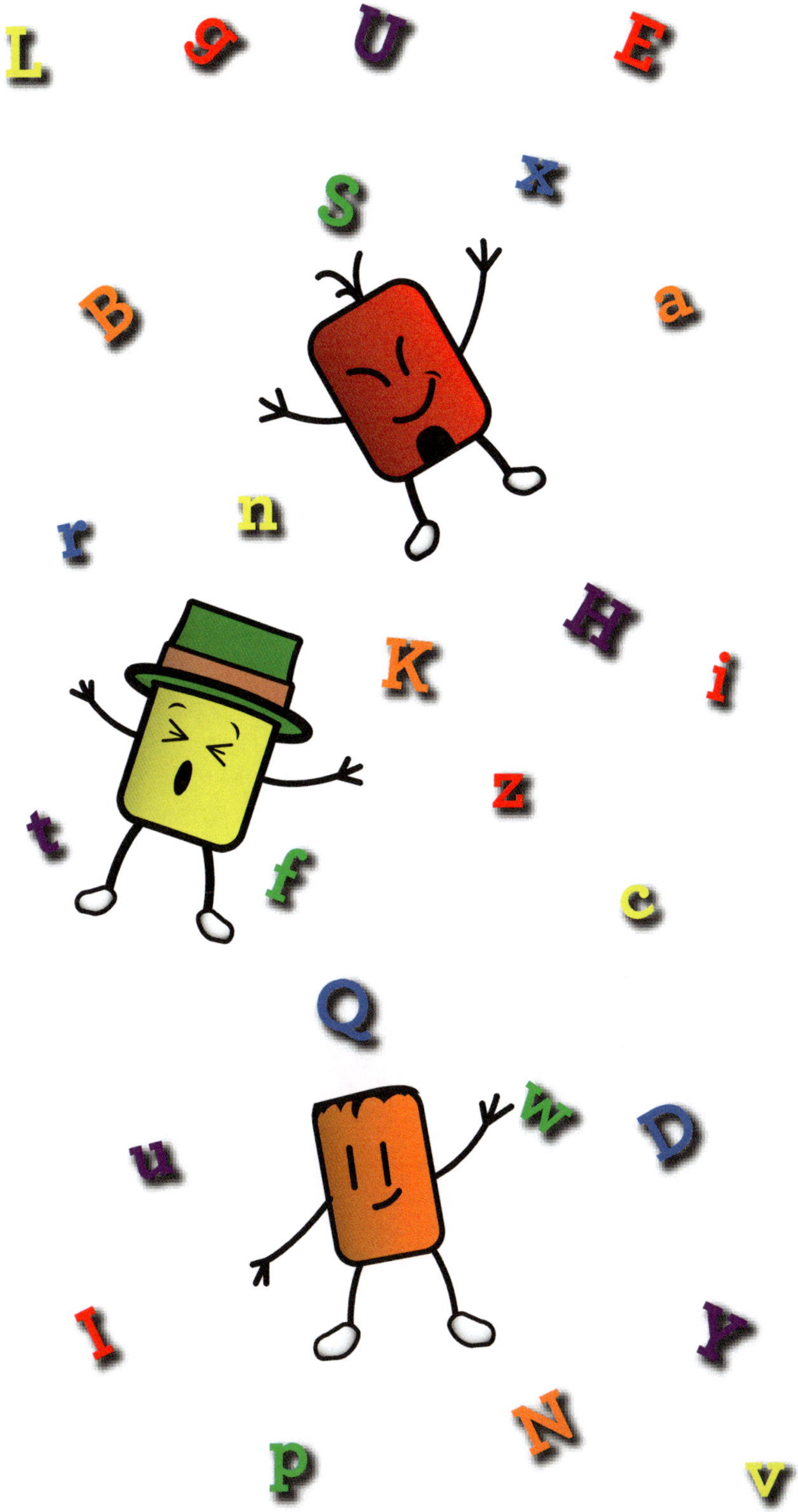

Want to learn more about the Lighties? Check out this book!

Where's Lighty?

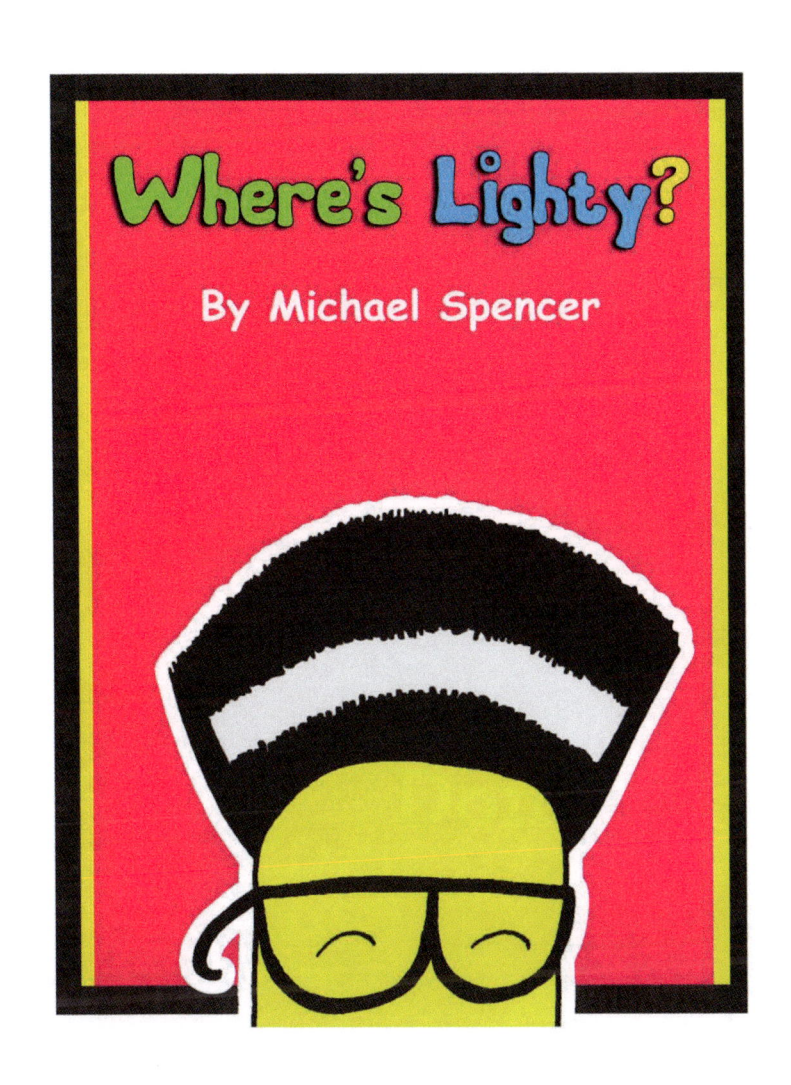

By Michael Spencer

Order now at
www.Lightyisland.com

Super Awesome Reader Award!

This award certifies that

_____

is now an ABC expert!

Date _____

Parent _____
Signature

Made in the USA
Charleston, SC
26 April 2016